RETIRED AND KILLIN' IT

The Ultimate Retirement Plan

Dethra,
   You were never really a contracted coach, you were a divine appointment for life-changing impact and new vision.
   Thank you for investing in me.
         Love,
           Lisa

Jethra,

You were never really a contracted coach, you were a divine appointment for life-changing impact and new vision. Thank you for investing in me.

Love,
[signature]

RETIRED AND KILLIN' IT

The Ultimate Retirement Plan

LISA J. HAYNES

Retired and Killin' It: The Ultimate Retirement Plan

Copyright © 2025 by Lisa J. Haynes

All rights reserved. No part of this publication may be reproduced, stored in a retrieval system, or transmitted in any form or by any means—electronic, mechanical, photocopy, recording, or otherwise—without the prior written permission of the publisher, except for brief quotations used in reviews or scholarly works.

The "KILLIN' IT"™ formula and related frameworks presented in this book are proprietary to the author. No part of this framework may be reproduced, shared, taught, or adapted for workshops, coaching programs, or commercial use without the author's express written consent.

While this book draws on real experiences, some names and details have been changed to protect the privacy of individuals. The content reflects the author's personal insights and experiences and is intended for informational and motivational purposes only. The author and publisher assume no responsibility for any outcomes resulting from the use of this material.

ISBN: 979-8-9875261-2-5
Library of Congress Number – 2025912390
Cataloging-in-Publication Data
Haynes, Lisa
Retired and Killin' It: The Ultimate Retirement Plan
Retirement—Psychological aspects. 2. Retirement—Social aspects.
Printed in the United States of America
Published by Dulles Publishing Company
44715 Prentice Drive #62
Ashburn, Virginia 20146
Editor: Kathy Savadel

Acknowledgments

All honor to God, my source and strength—none of this would be possible without Him.

To my husband, my biggest cheerleader and steadfast support—thank you for always being in my corner.

Thank you to my beta readers—*Katheryne Walker, Mary Hentges, Randy Haynes, and Digna Louis*—for reading quickly and offering thoughtful feedback on the manuscript.

To Marcia Davies, mPower founder and friend, who invited me to speak on a women's leadership panel for the Mortgage Bankers Association's *mPowering You* Conference—your invitation sparked the idea for *Retired and Killin' It*.

Jean and Maura Bradley, thanks for lunch in Sarasota and the nudge to keep pushing forward.

I'm blessed beyond measure to be surrounded by such love, faith, and fierce support.

- My mother, Bernice Payne—thank you for all you invested in me; here's another return on investment.

- My children—Michael (Anna), Gabrielle, Shekora, Asha, Diandra, Melinda, Tiffany, and Nicole—no matter what stage in life I'm in, to you, I will always be: Mom, Ma, Mum, and Mommala.

- My siblings—Eustace Jr., Teresa, Carla, Renee, Terri, and Karen (my sister/friend)—thank you for always having my back.

And in loving memory of my father, Eustace Sr., who often said, "When are you going to retire? You work so hard." Well, Dad—I did it!

Table of Contents

Acknowledgments i
Introduction v

Part 1: The Retirement Mindset Shift
Chapter 1: Know Your "Why" 1
Chapter 2: Identity & Reinvention 7

Part 2: KILLIN' IT - The Ultimate Retirement Plan
Chapter 3: K = Keep Moving 21
Chapter 4: I = Imagine What's Next 35
Chapter 5: L = Laugh a Lot 49
Chapter 6: L = Live for Legacy 59
Chapter 7: I = Ignite Your Passion 69
Chapter 8: N = Nurture Your Network 75
Chapter 9: I = Invest in Others 87
Chapter 10: T = Tell Yourself You Are KILLIN' IT ... 91

Part 3: Worksheets
APPENDIX: Retired and KILLIN' IT Worksheets . 105

Endnotes 121
About the Author 124

Introduction

Retirement—does that sound exciting, scary, or like a fog of uncertainty? Whether you're already there or planning to be soon, you deserve applause. You've worked hard and earned this next chapter. Retirement is supposed to be the reward. But for many, it doesn't feel like a reward at all.

Most people have focused on preparing financially for this moment for ten years or more. But what about everything else that retirement entails? What about the identity shift, the daily structure, the sense of purpose, the relationships, the joy? When we leave the company for the last time, are we ready for the next phase of life?

I found myself asking those same questions. After decades in finance leadership, I retired with a rough sketch of what was next: a little travel, time with my grandkids, and perhaps some consulting and coaching. However, I realized that I needed more than a rough sketch—I needed a road map.

That's where this book comes in. This isn't a financial book, and it's definitely not a boring checklist. It's a guide to the emotional, social, and identity shifts that come with retirement—the real stuff that makes this stage of your life either fulfilling or frustrating.

This book is a conversation about how you *really* do retirement—the emotional, social, physical, and spiritual side of it. It is the part that gets overlooked, but makes all the difference in whether this season feels full or just . . . quiet.

In the pages ahead, I'll introduce you to a simple but powerful framework I call the **KILLIN' IT** Formula: eight intentional ways to shape a retirement you enjoy.

Retirement isn't the end of your story; it's your next bold chapter—and you hold the pen. Let's get writing!

PART 1:
The Retirement Mindset Shift

Know Your "Why"

According to the Holmes–Rahe Life Stress Inventory,[1] retirement ranks tenth of the forty-three most stressful life events, higher than a significant change in a family member's health or a shift in your financial situation. That tells you everything you need to know. Retirement is a big deal, even when it's planned and welcomed.

So, the first question to ask yourself is: **Why?** What's my motivation for retiring?

Like any new season in life, knowing your "why" gives you a sense of direction. Whether you're getting married, changing jobs, or moving to a new state, clarifying your reasons can shape your decisions and help you manage the transition. Retirement is no different.

Maybe you've hit a mandatory retirement age and are stepping away because the calendar says it's time. Perhaps you're 55 and retiring early because you're financially able. You may be one of the unfortunate people who have been laid off because of downsizing or forced to take an early retirement package. Or you're stepping back because your health—or the health of someone you love—demands it. Each situation sets a different tone for what retirement might look like.

And that "why" matters. Retirement is not just about looking back at what you're leaving; it's about looking forward and choosing how you'll show up in this next chapter. Your "why" becomes your compass. It keeps you grounded when the excitement wears off or the voice in your head starts whispering, *"Now what?"*

Take Julie, for example. She was a government employee who retired at 58 with full benefits. Her "why" was simple: She'd worked 35 years and wanted freedom from work demands. But three months in, she was restless. Within a few months, she was back working part-time to have something to do. Her "why" answered only where she came from, not where she wanted to go. That's the trap: **When your "why" looks backward, it can't guide you forward.** Julie's story is a reminder: without a forward-looking why, retirement can feel aimless.

> Take a moment to write down your answers to these questions. There are no right or wrong responses—just real ones.
>
> - What's driving my decision to retire?

> - Am I moving toward something or just stepping away?
> - Is this the right time—or just the available time?

> 💡 **Pro Tip: Revisit your answers later. As your retirement evolves, so might your "why." That's normal. The goal is to keep checking in.**

My "why" was simple. Although I retired at 58 because my financial planner confirmed that I could, that was not my "why."

I asked myself, "Have you been successful in your career?" This led me to define *success*. I had been in my role for 10 years, and I felt I had accomplished all that I felt I wanted to. I made an impact and left a legacy—that was my definition of success. It was time to move on to the next chapter, expanding my influence and building on that foundation.

My "why" was that I had so much more to accomplish, and working full time was standing in the way. I might be exaggerating just a little...but not really. There's too much I still want to do, and that requires the freedom to do it.

Those who feel forced into retirement through a layoff or downsizing still need a "why." The loss of a job does not equal retirement because you have the choice to take on a new role or reinvent yourself doing something that may be very different from what you did in your career. However, if neither of those options appeals to you, that might be the beginning of finding your "why." When I retired, I knew that my assignment at the Mortgage Bankers Association was complete, and it was my lack of desire to start over at a new company that led me to think that retirement might be the best choice.

Your "why" doesn't have to be profound; it just needs to be **yours**. Finding conviction about your "why" is essential to your *KILLIN' IT* plan. It's about filling your life with what gives you purpose and brings you excitement.

What is your why?

_____
_____
_____
_____
_____
_____
_____
_____

Key Takeaways

_____
_____
_____
_____
_____
_____
_____
_____

When your "why" looks backward, it can't guide you forward.

Identity & Reinvention

For years—maybe decades—your answer to "What do you do?" probably came quickly:

- I'm the Chief Executive Officer
- I work in health care.
- I'm in public service (transit operator, government civil servant)
- I'm a business owner
- I'm in the Armed Services.

Whether you wore a suit, a badge, a uniform, or steel-toed boots, your work was part of how you saw yourself—and how others saw you.

But what happens when that identity is no longer tied to a title, a team, or a time clock? When there's no office, no more rounds, clients, customers, or schedule? What happens when someone asks, "What do you do?" and you're not quite sure how to answer?

I retired on September 30th, and in early October, I attended a women's summit with high-level executives from different industries. In preparing for the event, I knew I would meet people who would ask that inevitable question, "What do you do?" And for the first time in a while, I could not say, "CFO." When asked, I responded, "I just retired"—because truthfully, I didn't have anything else to say. Not yet.

Retirement isn't just the end of work. It's the beginning of a pivot—a shift from what you've always done to what you want to do next. It's a chance to reimagine your identity beyond the job and redefine what a fulfilling life looks like now.

Identity Shift

As you prepare for retirement, you need to evaluate and identify the "from what to what" transition. This is the psychological shift that requires us to focus on what's ahead while acknowledging what we leave behind. For some, the shift is easier because their job isn't fulfilling, but for many the satisfaction they get from their role makes the separation more difficult. Sociologist Helen Rose Fuchs Ebaugh introduced the concept of *role exit*, describing it as the process of disengaging from a role that is central to one's identity and establishing a new one that incorporates aspects of the former role. This transition can be emotionally challenging, and some retirees must navigate feelings of loss and uncertainty.[2]

I remember my decision to retire. The evaluation process was not lengthy. An executive coach asked me to reflect on a few questions to consider about what I wanted in my next role. After I completed the exercise she gave me, I realized I had no desire for another role; instead, I wanted to retire and do other things. I remember how much I smiled after the news of my retirement became public—it brought a sense of lightness that I didn't expect. However, I also recall the feeling when I shared the posting for my role on LinkedIn. It was sobering to realize that I would no longer be the Senior Vice President, Chief Financial Officer (CFO), and Chief Diversity & Inclusion Officer for the Mortgage Bankers Association (MBA). That title had a nice ring to it, but realizing I'd soon be trading it for "Retiree" took a minute to process. For a day or so, I experienced a few of the five stages of grief.

Grieving the Loss of Your Work Life

The Kübler-Ross model defines the five stages of grief as: (1) denial, (2) anger, (3) bargaining, (4) depression, and (5) acceptance.[3] Most of us are familiar with these concepts when grieving a loved one, but they can also apply to any major loss. The end of a career—voluntary or not—can have a strong emotional impact, and you shouldn't be

Identity & Reinvention

surprised if you find yourself moving through one or more of these stages.

For me, denial came in the form of disbelief. I kept asking myself, "Is this really happening?" Even though it was my choice to step into retirement, I could still remember the first day of my first job, and it didn't seem like it was over three decades ago. Sitting with the reasons why I decided to retire helped me move to acceptance. But that won't be the case for everyone.

Those who are pushed into retirement through downsizing, early retirement packages, or health challenges are more likely to experience a longer or deeper version of these stages. That's okay. It's part of the transition. If retirement came before you were ready, it can feel more like a door slamming shut than one opening. You may wrestle with grief, anger, or a sense of unfinished business—especially if your identity was closely tied to your role. Be gentle with yourself. This is a loss, and it deserves to be acknowledged.

But it's not the end of your value, your purpose, or your potential. Give yourself time to process what you didn't get to choose. Then, when you're ready, begin imagining what you can **choose** from here. Because you still have options. You still have power. And there's still a next chapter waiting to be written, **BY YOU.**

Transitioning to the "To"

After my brief grieving, I realized focusing on my "to" was essential to a healthy transition. A month later, I sat on a panel at MBA's mPowering You conference and told the audience, "I'm retired and killin' it." That moment sealed it. My "to" had become more exciting than my "from"—and I've never once looked back or missed my job titles.

The transition process will differ for each person, but the importance of identifying your "to" is the same. To begin the "from what to what" process, these two exercises will help you create your retirement mission statement and tagline.

> - Write a Retirement Mission Statement: a short reflection of your values and purpose, and what you want this season of your life to be about.
> - Create a Retirement Tagline: a line that makes you smile when someone asks, "So, what are you doing now?" It's your motto for this next chapter of your life.

I will share my own retirement statement and tagline so that you have an example to refer to as you approach the exercise.

> **My Retirement Mission Statement:** To use my gifts and abilities to continue to make a positive and lasting impact on the lives of others so that my legacy, which is every life I touch, extends beyond my lifetime.
>
> **My Retirement Tagline:** Retired and Killin' It!

Grab a pen, paper, or electronic device for this next section. There's no one correct answer here. What matters most is that it feels true to you.

> 💡 **Pro Tip:** Revisit your mission statement each year. Your values may stay the same, but your focus might evolve.

Part 1: Your Retirement Mission Statement

This is your compass. It doesn't have to be fancy—just honest. It should answer the following questions:

- Who am I now?
- What do I value most?
- How do I want to show up in this next chapter?
- What does "meaningful" look like to me?

Here's a formula to get your brain churning: "In this season of my life, I will focus on [*value or passion*], stay connected through [*activity or community*], and continue to grow by [*learning, giving, exploring, etc.*]."

> 💡 **Pro Tip:** Write it like you're talking to your future self, not like you're updating your résumé.

Part 2: Create Your Retirement Tagline

Try to distill it into one bold sentence or phrase—something you'd say when someone asks, "What do you do now?" Remember, it needs to make you smile when you say it.

What's the one-liner that captures how you want to live this next chapter of your life?

Here are some examples to get you started:

- "I'm retired, not expired."
- "I help people and grow tomatoes."
- "I finally have time for the things that matter."
- "I'm building a life I don't need a vacation from."
- "Fewer meetings, more meaning."

You've spent years introducing yourself based on a title that was assigned to you by an employer. Now you can create an introduction that speaks to your identity. While I served as CFO, people saw the title, but that was only part of the picture. It was my role, but who I was, and who I am, are so much more. That is the same for you. Create an introduction that gives people a vision they never expected of retirement.

> 💡 **Pro Tip:** *I know that this is not as easy as it reads, but a retirement coach, can be very helpful.*[4]

Now that you've had a chance to reflect on your "why," understand the shifts that come with retirement, and begin to reimagine your identity; you're ready for the framework that will guide the rest of the book. It's called the KILLIN' IT Formula, and it comprises eight key actions that will help you design a retirement that's bold, balanced, and uniquely yours.

Retirement Mission Statement

_____

_____

_____

_____

_____

_____

_____

Retirement Tagline

_____

_____

_____

_____

_____

_____

_____

You can create an introduction that speaks to your identity.

PART 2:
KILLIN' IT – The Ultimate Retirement Plan

KILLIN' IT!™
THE ULTIMATE RETIREMENT PLAN

K — Keep Moving (Physically, Mentally, and Socially)

I — Imagine What's Next (Dream Bold, Plan Smart)

L — Laugh a Lot (Find Joy in Everyday Moments)

L — Live for Legacy (Make an Impact and Share Your Wisdom)

I — Ignite Your Passion (Pursue What Brings You Energy and Fulfillment)

N — Nurture Your Network (Cultivate Meaningful and Inspiring Relationships)

I — Invest in Others (Share Knowledge and Give Back)

T — Tell Yourself You Are Killin' It! (Own Your Retirement with Confidence)

www.retiredandkillinit.com

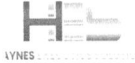

Copyright Haynes Executive Solutions, 2025

Retirement isn't the end of your story; it's your next bold chapter.

K = Keep Moving
(Physically, Mentally, Socially)

Let's be real, retirement doesn't come with an instruction manual. One week, you dream of morning workouts, golf outings, and midday naps. Next, you're staring at the ceiling thinking, *Now what?* That's where "K" comes in: Keep Moving.

Most of us have delusions of grandeur when we think of retired life, such as working out twice daily to get fit, or growing vegetables in the backyard to be super healthy. But the reality is, you can get used to not being stressed—and fast. Think about it: You've been on the move for thirty or forty years, grinding it out daily, and now you can take control and do absolutely nothing. That is precisely what I did for the first week or two after I retired. Other than going to the gym (which absolutely does constitute moving), I cannot tell you what I did because nothing comes to mind. It felt fantastic not to have to do anything at all. But the novelty wore off fast: By the third week, I

K = Keep Moving

realized it was time to put my plan in place—the sofa was no place to begin KILLIN' IT.

K (Keep Moving) is foundational to your plan. Moving is the best defense against the dark side of retirement: the negative aspects and challenges that individuals may face after leaving the workforce. Think of it like gravity—retirement naturally pulls us toward stillness, isolation, and decline unless we actively and deliberately push back. These issues can significantly affect the mental health, physical well-being, and overall quality of life of retirees.

The Dark Side of Retirement

Here are some interesting and jarring statistics from the Retirement Manifesto website:

- 60% of people retire earlier than planned, often because of health problems, disability, or caregiving responsibilities.
- 50% are driven to retirement because of health problems or disability.
- 25% retired because they had to take care of their spouse or family member.
- 20% were forced into retirement because of downsizing at their companies.

- Retirement increases the probability of depression by approximately 40%.[5]

According to the National Council on Aging,

- 1%–5% of older adults living in the general community experience major depression.
- 11.5% of older adults who are hospitalized suffer from depression.
- 13.5% of older adults who require home health care experience depression.[6]

In addition, Senior Living.org reports that alcohol remains the most common substance for which older adults seek treatment, followed by heroin.[7]

I provide these facts not to depress you and scare you, but to help you position yourself and your plan to minimize or eliminate these factors. Retired or not, knowledge is power. The message that **retirement is all gloss and no grit** is only half the story—it tells the headline and skips the footnotes.

Moving Physically

The benefits of physical movement seem obvious. According to AARP, "By the time you reach your 50s, your strength, balance, and endurance are already beginning to wane." Seriously, 50? AARP also reports on a study published in

K = Keep Moving

the *Journals of Gerontology* that revealed that "both men and women in their 50s began to slip in their ability to stand on one leg and rise from a chair, and that declines continued into the next decades."[8] I was disturbed and slightly offended by reading this, but I did not attempt the exercise in case I failed.

The average retirement age is still hovering around 62 (although people are working longer), but even when we are working and moving, we continue to lose muscle mass. If we don't actively fight against physical decline, it's a lost battle. The good news is that some physical deterioration, when deliberately attacked, can be reversed.

Finally, a study conducted by the National Institute on Aging concluded that older adults with declining physical function are at a greater risk of dying.[9] However, in contrast, *Medical News Today* reported on a study in which participants who increased their physical activity reduced their risk of heart attack and stroke by 11%, compared with participants who reduced their exercise and increased their risk by 27%. What kind of activity was involved in this study? Moderate to vigorous activity three to four days a week for twenty to thirty minutes.[10]

Think about how much time you have each week in retirement. Assuming you're awake twelve hours a day, seven days a week (and most people are awake even longer), four days of exercise at 30 minutes a day adds up to just 120 minutes—or 2 out of your 84 waking hours. That's only 2% of your total time awake. Your body isn't asking for much to keep you on the healthier side of the ledger.

Your Retirement Time versus Movement Time
Awake Time = 84 hours/week

Activity	Hours/Week	% of Awake Time
Physical activity (30 min, 4x)	2 hours	2.4
Watching TV (3.0 hours/day)	21 hours	25
Napping/resting (2.5 hours/day)	17.5 hours	21
Socializing/phone calls (2 hours/day)	14 hours	17
Online/screen time (1.5 hours/day)	10.5 hours	12.5

Here is my story: I worked out regularly before retiring, but it was not planned or targeted. I aimed for three to four days a week, mostly cardio, and occasionally I used the leg weight machines.

It was my Dad who inspired me to step up my game. He had a massive stroke that paralyzed his right side, and although he could not walk, his mental faculties were fully intact. I would speak to my Dad on the phone, because he lived in another state, and he would ask if I had ridden my bike or gone to the gym that day. He encouraged

K = Keep Moving

me to keep exercising so my body would remain healthy as I aged.

I know what lies in my family genes: high blood pressure, gout, heart disease, kidney disease, and a history of stroke. I implore you to know what's in yours so that you can be proactive in fighting against it. My Dad's death inspired me to get a personal trainer—a decision that changed everything. My personal trainer is my investment in me, and she has added discipline to my routine, helped me regain muscle, and adjusted my diet. She knows that I believe life is too short to eat rabbit food and that dessert is my favorite meal of the day. However, she has taught me how to balance what I like to eat against what I need to eat.

You have only one body, and you are 100% responsible for it. Invest in yourself! To enjoy retirement, it is crucial to maintain good physical health. If you're facing physical challenges, there are still great options, like chair yoga or seated step machines. In the chapters that follow, as you create your plan, prioritize how you will keep it moving physically. Going to the gym may not be for you, but studies show that walking 8,000 steps daily can improve cardiovascular health. Find a physical activity you enjoy and find someone to hold you accountable. But whatever you do, keep moving. My self-imposed rule is that I do not allow myself to stay in the house more than one day unless I am sick.

Moving Mentally

Our brain is a muscle. Use it or lose it.

This is not always easy to admit, but specific health challenges are associated with mental decline. According to a research and education organization called the BMJ Group, our cognitive functional decline can start as early as age 45. That's the dark side to retirement, mentally speaking. Our mental abilities are on the decline. This is not something to dwell on or obsess about, but it is something to be aware of because to KILL IT, we must fight against the dark side.

Exercising the Brain

When we work, we actively use our mental faculties, but when we retire the challenges that push our brains are no longer present, and our brain muscles are no longer exercised to the same degree. We still have it, but we're not using it, and if we go too long without it, we lose it. However, this does not have to be the case.

In the Chapter 4, you'll have a chance to envision your retirement, and you'll decide whether you want to work during your retirement or whether you want to be 100% retired. In either case, you must keep your mind active. How actively you do so is up to you. Whether you have

K = Keep Moving

a PhD or a GED, your mind wants to be stimulated. For example, although I love a good medical or legal television series, this stimulation does not feed the brain enough, and binge watching a show works against the physical element that we just conquered.

Your retirement plan must consider how you will remain mentally active. Crossword puzzles and word-finds are ways to keep your mind active, but much more is available to help you challenge your mind. Consider teaching or tutoring in your field of expertise to stay sharp while giving back. My mother, in her 80s, provides tutoring to individuals in English as a second language at the local library. There are also many "Brain Boosters"[11] to keep your mind firing on all cylinders.

> **Brain Boosters**
>
> - **Lumosity:** An app, designed by neuroscientists, that offers daily games that target memory, attention, flexibility, speed, and problem-solving (*www.lumosity.com/landing*)
> - **Duolingo:** Offers lessons to help you learn a new language (or brush up on one from high school) (*www.duolingo.com*)
> - **MasterClasses:** High-quality video classes taught by experts and celebrities in fields ranging from science and writing to cooking and negotiation (www.masterclass.com)
> - **Coursera or edX:** Free and paid online courses from top universities (e.g., Yale, Stanford, MIT) (*www.coursera.org* or *www.edx.org*)
> - **NYT Games or AARP's Staying Sharp:** Classic brain teasers, such as crosswords, Sudoku, and word games; AARP's platform even has guided programs for mental wellness and mindfulness. (https://www.nytco.com/products/games/ or https://stayingsharp.aarp.org/)

Keeping Up

Leaving the workforce means you are no longer on the cutting edge of whatever is evolving in the industry you left. However, being retired means we have all the time we never had while we were working to learn more about what interests us—cutting-edge or not. In this case, you're not learning to become an expert in the field; you're learning to remain relevant and challenge your mind.

No matter what era you grew up in, things will have changed dramatically by the time you retire. For example: complete sentences feel like a thing of the past. Now, keeping up with younger generations means decoding a whole new language of texts, abbreviations, and inside shorthand that barely resemble traditional conversation. Don't be the person that the Southwest Airlines flight attendants joked about needing an 8-year-old to help connect to the Wi-Fi. As we age, our brains won't be able to process all the changing technology as quickly as when we were younger, but mentally challenging ourselves when we leave full-time work is essential.

Just as moving physically works against the decline in our bodies, we want to fight against allowing our brains to become lazy and stagnant.

Moving Socially

In Chapter 8, we will dive deeper into the notion of social networks and the process of fostering relationships. What is key for the foundation of a good retirement is that, as you build your plan, you should include a social component, because there is a dark side to the social component as well.

According to the Certified Professional Retirement Coaching Association (CPRC), "Research suggests that while a client is working, they can have up to 22 high-quality (face-to-face) interactions with people daily. When people retire, that number can get cut in half, to 11, and those interactions are generally of lesser quality because they are more likely to be by phone or email rather than face-to-face."[12] The result of this reality is that loneliness has an opening to creep in.

The CPRC also identified various studies on loneliness, suggesting that

- 40% of Americans don't feel close to others,
- Loneliness shortens the life span twice as much as obesity (Dr. John Cacioppo), and
- Loneliness also affects the body.

"Loneliness triggers a state of hyper-vigilance. A lonely brain is on the lookout for social threats, which consequently puts us on the defensive. We become more reactive to adverse events and perceive daily hassles as more stressful."[13]

Being aware of the dark side and its realities provides valuable insights for creating an effective attack plan. Dr. Charles Swindoll wrote a book titled, *Life is 10% what*

K = Keep Moving

happens to you and 90% how you react to it.[14] Your ability to stay active socially is your response to the dark side.

Consider the following as ways you can keep moving socially:

- Join a club
- Start a club
- Sign up for a class
- Regularly schedule connections
- Volunteer
- Teach

Keep Moving Recap

To fight the quiet pitfalls of retirement and keep thriving, build movement into your plan in all three areas:

PHYSICALLY

- ✓ Aim for at least thirty minutes of moderate activity, three to four days per week.
- ✓ Walking 8,000 steps a day improves cardiovascular health.
- ✓ Know your family health history and create a prevention plan.
- ✓ Consider working with a trainer or finding a fitness buddy.

MENTALLY

- ✓ Challenge your brain through learning, puzzles, or conversation.
- ✓ Try an app like Lumosity, MasterClass, or Duolingo.
- ✓ Stay curious—even 20 minutes of mental activity a day helps.
- ✓ Learn something new to keep up with the grandkids.

SOCIALLY

- ✓ Aim for meaningful, face-to-face interactions.
- ✓ Join or start a club, take a class, or volunteer regularly.
- ✓ Schedule time with friends and family.
- ✓ Don't wait for invitations: Create the connection.

> 💡 **Pro Tip**: Your retirement plan isn't just about saving money; it's about keeping your mind, body, and spirit healthy.

Now that you understand the importance of movement, let's put this knowledge in motion. In the next chapter, you'll begin crafting a retirement vision that reflects rest and reinvention.

What will you do to remain active?

_____

_____

_____

_____

_____

_____

_____

I = Imagine What's Next
(Dream Bold, Plan Smart)

This is where the work begins. Reading about a plan is a start, but it's not a plan. You must create the plan. As a Certified Professional Retirement Coach, I spend hours helping people draft the plan that excites them to move out of full-time employment into *retired-ish* and KILLIN' IT. I love watching the light come on when someone realizes that what's ahead is far more exciting than what they've been holding onto. So, let's cut to the chase and get to work.

Not Everyone Starts from the Same Place

As you start imagining what's next, it's important to acknowledge that retirement looks different for everyone. Some people have the financial freedom to explore new hobbies or travel. Others may still need to work part-time, care for aging loved ones, or have not retired by choice.

You might be entering this next chapter of your life at age 70 instead of 60, or you've never felt tied to a specific

I = Imagine What's Next

career, but now that you're out of the workforce you feel a little untethered.

That's okay. There's no one right way to do this.

Whether you're designing your dream chapter or just trying to find a rhythm that works, the KILLIN' IT formula still applies. This isn't about status—it's about creating meaning, joy, and connection with what you have, where you are.

Start small. Dream anyway.

❖❖❖❖❖

Getting Creative with Retirement: Your Possibilities, Bucket, and Dare Lists

In this section, you'll start getting creative with your retirement. Don't overthink it. Your lists will grow and evolve with time. Instead of just asking, "How will I fill my time?" consider this: "What have I never given myself permission to try?"

You'll create three lists—Possibilities, Bucket, and Dare—to help you dream bigger, push your limits, and maybe even surprise yourself. If you're not in a space where you can spend fifteen uninterrupted minutes, flag the page and return to it. You don't want to cheat yourself on this exercise because it's fun and helps you identify possibilities you didn't realize were available. It's also foundational for creating your plan. Make three columns to create your three lists.

- **Possibilities List:**
    - *What are some things you've thought about doing but never explored?*
    - *These could be hobbies, topics, languages, places, or experiences. There is no pressure to create a long list but allow your mind to run free to discover what sparks your interest.*
        ★ List as many as you like.
- **Bucket List:**
    - *What do you want to do before you die?*
    - *These are your bucket list dreams—big or small, serious or silly.*
        ★ Write down at least five.
- **Dare List:**
    - *What bold thing(s) will you dare yourself to do?*
    - *Something that slightly scares you.*
    - *This is your challenge to take a leap. Stretch outside your comfort zone.*
        ★ Pick one to two and be specific.

I = Imagine What's Next

Possibilities	Bucket	Dare

> 💡 **Pro Tip: You will find a copy of this in the appendix or go to www.retiredandkillinit.com for the full workbook.**

It is worth taking a break and revisiting your lists later because you may think of more items. Once you are comfortable that you've exhausted your list, begin with the Possibilities List and identify the things you are curious enough to explore further. You may have considered rock climbing, but you're not interested in the physical training and the investment required to get started. Like me, you may be interested in learning a foreign language, or in my case, relearning the Spanish I learned in high school, but you don't have the discipline or the passionate desire to do it. Don't choose things because they seem like a good idea. Choose things that excite you. Remember, this next phase of life is about doing whatever you want.

Next are the items on your Bucket List. Bucket List items often require financial, mental, or physical commitment. They are not part of our everyday lives, so we need to plan for them. Your Bucket List items are attainable goals, but they need to be appropriately planned because it may not be fiscally savvy to try to conquer them all in Years 1 and 2. If you have more than five items on your Bucket List, consider ranking them based on their importance to you.

Finally, we have the Dare List. Something on this list should be so big that it's scary. You have considered it, mulled it over, and debated it in your head for some time, but fear looms overhead like a storm cloud. If you have more than two items on this list, consider whether your dare is big enough. Tackling the items on your Dare List will come at a cost. If the goal is big enough, it might stir up things like:

- Fear of failure
- Fear of rejection

I = Imagine What's Next

- Fear of success
- Fear of judgment
- Fear of the unknown

I'm a person of faith and a Christian. The idea of choosing faith instead of fear is a foundational biblical teaching. Still, fear is a real and valid emotion, regardless of your beliefs. It can't be dismissed or wished away. The Dare List encourages you to recognize the fear and move forward anyway, even if you're scared. I believe courage and calling can exist in the same space as uncertainty.

And that brings me to my Dare List—you're reading it. This isn't just a book; it's part of a bigger vision and mission to encourage you to rethink retirement and reimagine what comes next. Who am I to think I can redefine retirement? There are many resources available to assist retirees, and retirement is personal—there's no one-size-fits-all. But the better question to ask is: Why not?

Every big success starts as an idea in someone's mind, and every failure teaches a lesson. Before you dismiss one of your dares as impossible, ask yourself: What's the worst thing that could happen? Even if the only outcome of my dare is that one person reads this book and builds a better retirement plan, that's success in my eyes.

Stretch Your Vision: Dream Beyond the Lists

Now that you've brainstormed your Possibilities, Bucket, and Dare Lists, it's time to stretch that vision further. What else could retirement look like if you gave yourself full permission to dream? What would you do if you had all the time and money you needed? Would you:

- Write a memoir or start a blog?
- Learn to paint, DJ, or salsa dance?
- Train for a fitness goal—at any age?
- Create a YouTube channel to share your expertise?
- Spend a month living somewhere new?
- Turn a hobby into a side hustle?
- House swap (i.e., trade homes with someone abroad for a month or two, and live like a local)?
- Try your hand at stand-up comedy?

You've spent a career thinking practically. Now is the time to think playfully, even outrageously. I read a story about a man who, after years of saving and frugal living, retired at 58 with a modest sum of money and a dream of traveling the world. He spent a year backpacking through Southeast Asia, focusing on experiencing culture and local life rather than lavish accommodations. He proved that a fulfilling travel journey can be achieved on a limited

I = Imagine What's Next

budget. Although backpacking anywhere is not my idea of fun, I love that he followed through on his dare.

The Big Picture

Now that you've explored how you'll keep moving and mapped out your Possibilities, Bucket, and Dare Lists, you're ready to envision retirement in a fuller context. Before diving into the details of your plan, take a moment to sketch a big-picture view. Create a pie chart that illustrates how you plan to allocate your time in retirement. This should provide a broad overview of the categories described in the following illustration. We'll dig into more detail in later chapters.

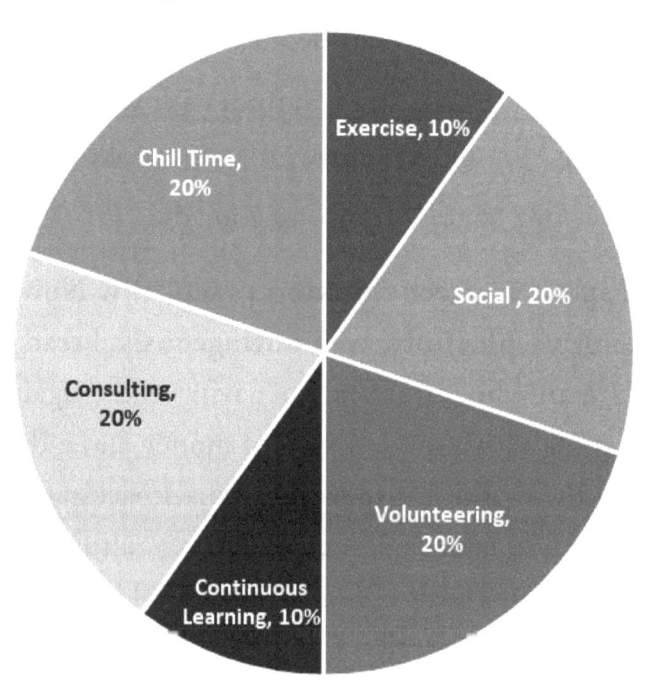

- Exercise, 10%
- Social, 20%
- Volunteering, 20%
- Continuous Learning, 10%
- Consulting, 20%
- Chill Time, 20%

Although a pie chart is not a commitment, it gives you some idea of how you want to spend your time in retirement, but it's very high level. Let's drill down.

Building on Chapter 2, where we looked at "from-what-to-what," in this next section we'll compare, side by side, what life looked like in the "from" and what life will look like in the "to."

◆◆◆◆◆

Old Structure versus New Rhythm

Choose a weekday that represents a typical day for you, recognizing that no one day is precisely the same but that commonalities do exist. Complete the following chart (included in the appendix as well in the full workbook at www.retiredandkillinit.com).

	Pre-Retirement Life	Post-Retirement Life
Morning	Up at 6:00 a.m., 1-hour commute, arrive at work at 9:00 a.m., coffee and emails, staff meeting	Morning: coffee in bed and get up at 9:00 a.m., watch the morning shows, go for a walk with a friend, or go to the gym

I = Imagine What's Next

	Pre-Retirement Life	Post-Retirement Life
Afternoon	Lunch, meetings, seeing patients	Meet friends for a 2-hour lunch, do some shopping, work on a craft or your consulting business, take a nap
Evening	1-hour commute, grocery store, prepare and eat dinner, back online for work, reading, watching TV, prepare for next day, bed	Take a cooking class, prepare dinner or go to dinner, take an evening stroll, attend an evening event, relax in bed

The first column lists what you *had* to do. The second column lists what you *want* to do. Here is where you start thinking about what excites, relaxes, fulfills, and encourages you. If a particular activity doesn't make you happy, or you don't want to do it, then it should not be in the right-hand column. Yes, there are things, like doctors' appointments, that we must do for our own sake, but the number of "must-do" items in the right-hand column should be limited.

The one thing you discover quickly in retirement is that Saturday becomes Monday–Friday. But having six Saturdays can be challenging because it entails more time on your hands than you realize, so we drill the ideal day into the perfect week.

The concept for this exercise mirrors the ideal day, but now you can map out a week that excites you. Your challenge is to avoid the rinse-and-repeat cycle. You've been on a schedule for decades, doing almost the same thing every day. Now, you can wake up each day and make it your own. Think outside the box. Return to your lists (Possibilities, Bucket, Dare) and fit those items in. Flip back to "Keep Moving" (Chapter 3) and ensure you've included the activities you have committed to from there. Don't short yourself. My retirement coaching clients build their excitement in this section. If you're not excited yet, find a retirement coach to help you get there.

	Pre-Retirement Life	Post-Retirement Life
Monday	Coffee/breakfast, work, lunch, work, commute, family events, dinner, bed	Waiting for a new plan
Tuesday	Coffee/breakfast, work, lunch, work, commute, family events, dinner, bed	Unscheduled
Wednesday	Coffee/breakfast, work, lunch, work, commute, family events, dinner, bed	Pending Purpose

I = Imagine What's Next

	Pre-Retirement Life	Post-Retirement Life
Thursday	Coffee/breakfast, work, lunch, work, commute, family events, dinner, bed	Time to Fill
Friday	Coffee/breakfast, work, lunch, work, commute, family events, dinner, bed	Undefined (for now)
Saturday	Household chores, family obligations, catching up on things not done during the week	Household chores, family obligations, catching up on things not done during the week
Sunday	Church, brunch, nap, family time, dinner, bed	Church, brunch, nap, family time, dinner, bed

To Work or Not to Work? That Is the Question

Retirement doesn't have to mean zero work. For some people, work is part of their joy and rhythm. The questions you need to ask yourself concerning work are:

- Why am I going to work?
- What are my terms?
- What do I want to do?

Deciding how work will play a role in your retirement is essential. According to a blog on the Eastcastle Place website, 52% of older adults who consider getting a job do so because they are bored. But boredom isn't the only reason to work—for many, it's also about purpose, people, structure, or fun. You control your time, energy, and joy by deciding why and how you want to work now.

Don't rush this section. Come back to it with fresh eyes in a day or two. Each time you revisit your plan, you'll see it more clearly. The most exciting thing about retirement? It's yours to design. And it gets better the more you dare to imagine.

This is where the magic starts. But listen, all the planning in the world won't matter if you forget to enjoy it.

Next up: laughter. Not the polite kind, but the deep, joyful, laugh 'til you cry kind. Because fun isn't a bonus in retirement—it's fuel. Let's talk about how to build more of *that* into your life.

Moving is the best defense against the dark side of retirement.

L = Laugh a Lot
(Find Joy in Everyday Moments)

Let me make a point that bears repeating: Retirement isn't just about financial planning and doctor's appointments. It's also about fun. About joy. About laughing so hard that your face and your stomach hurt.

You've spent years being serious, productive, and responsible. And although those things still have their place, now's the time to make room for lightness, ridiculous belly laughs, and everyday joy that doesn't need a reason.

That kind of laughter isn't just feel-good—it is good for you.

Several published studies have argued that laughter is a strong medicine. A study published by the Mayo Clinic confirms what we already know in our gut: Laughter is powerful. A good laugh makes us feel better. In the short term, it boosts oxygen to the brain, releases endorphins, and relaxes the body. Over time, it improves immunity, relieves pain, and even helps combat stress and anxiety.

L = Laugh a Lot

Laughter lowers blood pressure, soothes tension, and triggers your body's natural painkillers. It's a full-body wellness treatment—and it's free.

> No matter how serious life gets, you still gotta have that one person you can be completely crazy with.

So, if you've ever felt guilty about watching funny videos on social media, calling your funniest friend, or rewatching your favorite sitcom to laugh out loud, don't. That joy isn't a distraction from retirement; it's part of the plan. There is nothing better than a side-splitting belly laugh.

Find Funny People

I love to laugh and make others laugh. I've always had a quick wit and can respond quickly. Throughout my career, I have frequently used humor to convey my point or alleviate tension in the room. Sometimes, I crack myself up. But I have a friend who can make me belly laugh like no one else. No matter how bad things are, we can always find something to laugh about. I'll refrain from sharing stories because "what happens in Vegas, stays in Vegas." But I think you need someone with whom you can drop all pretenses and remove the mask of adulthood.

Having a good friend in your life whom you can count on to bring laughter is important because life will get tough. Not only do you have someone who can make you laugh even when you don't want to, but you have memories to draw on of moments when that belly laughter soothed your soul.

Don't Take Yourself Too Seriously

We all know that one person who corrects everything, never misses a beat, and treats every mistake like a crisis. Don't be that person, especially not with yourself.

One of the secrets to laughing more is simply giving yourself permission to mess up and move on. Eventually, you'll walk into a room and forget why you went there. Or spend fifteen minutes looking for your glasses only to realize they're on your head. Forget a name. Tell the same story twice. Welcome to the club.

L = Laugh a Lot

Call them senior moments if you want—I call them an *earned prerogative*. You've earned the right to laugh at life. You're choosing joy over judgment every time you chuckle instead of cringe. That's freedom. Laugh, smile, shrug, and move on. Life's too short to spend energy ruminating on minor incidents. And you must admit, looking for your cell phone while you're talking on it is funny.

Eliminate Negativity

An old song recorded by Bing Crosby and the Andrews Sisters back in 1944 provides solid advice for the second act.

> **You've got to accentuate the positive.**
> **Eliminate the negative**
> **Latch on to the affirmative.**
> **Don't mess with Mr. In-Between.**

Our happiness is closely tied to cultivating a positive mindset. Negative thinking is like cancer: It spreads unless it's stopped in its tracks. I find negative people exhausting.

As we get older, we become less flexible and agile, but if we are not careful, we become a "Negative Nancy" or "Negative Norman" (for short, NN) who can find something to complain about no matter what is going on. You may be reading this and thinking, "This does not apply to me," but being an NN applies to everyone at some point. Whether it's because we've had a long day, are in pain, depressed, or simply unhappy at that moment or period in life, we all go through phases of complaining. Does your complaining phase last for minutes, hours, days, or the rest of your lifetime? Most of us know when we are in a negative mood because we start to get on our nerves.

Wondering if you've slipped into Negative Nancy/Norman mode? Watch for these signs:

- People stop responding when you start complaining. If, after your second or third comment, you receive no response from those accompanying you, they hope that you'll stop talking if they stay silent.

- If each time you make a comment, someone counters your comment with something that takes a more positive perspective on the situation or changes the subject, you're probably in that negative space.

- There's a sense of joy being sucked out of the room when you start talking and you notice people giving each other the eye. READ THE ROOM!

You are responsible for monitoring yourself, and life is too short to spend it complaining. Learn to course-correct when you sense yourself slipping into a dark hole of

L = Laugh a Lot

negativity. If you lack the self-awareness to recognize it, be open to friends who want to help you.

Play Outside Again

Somewhere along the road to adulthood, most of us lost our ability to play. As kids, our primary goal was to maximize our daily playtime. As a child growing up in the city, the summers were filled with playing outside all day, from sunup to sundown when we were not in camp. The classic parental line in my neighborhood was "Don't let the streetlights beat you home." In other words, you were expected to be in the house before your parents could see the streetlights. I have no idea what we did outside from 8:00 a.m. to 8:00 p.m., but we weren't bored. And we did not go home for a break because we risked being told to stay in the house.

As we grow up, somehow, the concept of playing becomes immature. We no longer take time to play; even our games are serious. Golf is supposed to be a game but try clowning around on the golf course and see how that works out for you.

> **Maturity is overrated.
> Go outside and play!**

Retirement is the perfect opportunity to reinvent the notion of "go outside to play." That probably doesn't mean a bountiful game of tag or touch football (although if you're up for it, don't let age stop you), but checkers in the park should not be the definition of adult play. I love hearing adults say they are going to a Disney park and have no children with them. Why not scream on the roller coaster or get soaking wet on the raging rapids ride? Remind yourself of what you enjoyed as a child and reinvent it.

I recall a trip I took to Florida some years ago when the group of adults with whom my husband and I were traveling found a park with go-kart racing. It's incredible how competitive adults are, regardless of whether there's a prize to be won. When we boarded our vehicles, an onlooker would have thought this was the Indy 500. We were all very serious, and when the light turned green, it was game on: Pedals slammed down to the floor. We laughed about that experience for the rest of the day. Although that was more than a decade ago, I would do it again today with the same enthusiasm.

Try Something that Scares You (a Little)

Remember the Possibilities List you created earlier? Here's an excellent opportunity to find something on the list that's fun and takes you out of your comfort zone. When you try something new—especially something you're a little afraid of looking silly doing—you make space for joy to surprise you.

Take a dance class. Go zip-lining. Audition for community theater. Learn improv. You don't have to be good at it; you simply must show up with curiosity and a willingness to laugh at yourself. And if others laugh at you, it's okay; maybe you gave them joy. The goal isn't to become fearless. The goal is to laugh in the face of fear. The goal is KILLIN' IT.

❖❖❖❖❖

This Week's Joy Challenge

This week, do something purely for the joy of it. Watch a comedy. Call your funniest friend. Dance in your kitchen.

Ride a bike with no destination. Say yes to something that makes you feel silly, young, or slightly ridiculous.

You've been productive your whole life—now give joy a turn.

Retirement is serious business, but in the next chapter you'll learn that finding your joy turns it into fun. Joy isn't an extra benefit—it's essential. It keeps us light. Connected. Alive.

And the next chapter explains how it just might be the best investment you make.

"Retirement is the perfect opportunity to reinvent the notion of "go outside to play."

L = Live for Legacy
(Make an Impact and Share Your Wisdom)

> *You have no idea what your legacy will be.*
> *Your legacy is what you do every day.*
> *Your legacy is every life you've touched, every person whose life was either moved or not.*
> *It's every person you've harmed or helped.*
> *That's your legacy.*
> —Maya Angelou

While imagining what's next, we must consider the end game. Our legacy is part of our why. Legacy goes beyond what you will leave for your children. Yes, your children and their children are part of your legacy, but it's bigger than that. As Dr. Angelou indicates, a legacy can be positive or negative. Your legacy is your choice, and by not choosing, you are making the decision that it doesn't matter.

L = Live for Legacy

Legacy Defined

Merriam-Webster defines *legacy* as "something transmitted by or received from an ancestor or predecessor or the past (https://www.merriam-webster.com/dictionary/legacy)."

The *Oxford English Dictionary* (*Oxford*) also adds: "A legacy is something handed down by a predecessor, often in the form of a lasting influence, reputation, or contribution (https://www.oed.com/dictionary/legacy_n?tl=true)."

The *Merriam-Webster* definition is a traditional version that assumes a relationship exists between the giver of the legacy and the receiver. *Oxford* is also conventional in its definition, adding the forms that legacy might take, such as lasting influence, reputation, or contribution. I like how ChatGPT's artificial intelligence algorithm combined these two to create a more modern definition: the legacy that fits those who are Retired and Killin' It:

> Legacy is the lasting impact an individual leaves on others or on society, through their actions, contributions, character, and values. It is how one is remembered and the influence that continues after their active presence is gone.

It's essential to note that legacy can be either positive or negative. Some people are remembered for their compassion and contributions; others, for the harm they caused or the trust they broke. The point is—every action, every choice leaves a mark.

Some legacies are tied to the people's work while living, leaving a positive impact on society or in the lives of others. For example:

- **Rosa Parks:** Sparked the Montgomery Bus Boycott by not giving up her seat, became a symbol of civil rights, and advanced the rights of Black Americans.

- **Michael Jackson:** Revolutionized global pop culture through music, dance, and performance; his music crossed cultures, ages, and races, uniting people worldwide. He broke racial barriers on MTV, transformed music videos into art forms ("Thriller" alone revolutionized the industry), and set a new standard for live performance.

- **Steve Jobs:** Revolutionized technology and design, changing how the world communicates, works, and creates through Apple's innovation. Today, Apple continues to be a dominant leader in communications.

Others used their retirement to build upon or expand their legacy. For example:

- **Maya Angelou:** Even after retiring from formal teaching and touring, she continued writing,

L = Live for Legacy

mentoring young artists, and speaking publicly into her later years, deepening her influence on literature, civil rights, and culture.

- **Jimmy Carter:** After leaving the presidency, he built an even bigger legacy through humanitarian work with Habitat for Humanity, global health initiatives, and human rights advocacy. His post-retirement accomplishments arguably became his most admired contribution.

- **Dick Hoyt:** After retiring from his regular job, he and his son Rick (who had cerebral palsy) completed hundreds of marathons and triathlons together, inspiring millions with their message of perseverance and unconditional love. As a native Bostonian, I recall watching the duo participate in the Boston Marathon for many years, and they were a great source of inspiration.

- **Juanita Gray:** In her second act, she worked for the Denver Public Library, focusing on outreach to the Black community. She was instrumental in creating a tutoring program at Warren Library, where fourth graders who weren't reading at their class level were tutored by eighth graders considered underachievers themselves. Her efforts significantly influenced literacy and community engagement in Denver.

The AARP Foundation supports this through its **Experience Corps** initiative, which engages adults aged 50 and older as literacy tutors for struggling students in public schools. It's a powerful way for retirees to continue making a meaningful impact on education across the country.

No matter what you are retiring from or where you are moving to, you have a legacy that will continue beyond your working years. You still have something that the world needs. It may feel small to you, but it could be everything to someone else. You might be the best hype person on the planet. I can guarantee you that someone in your six degrees of separation needs to be hyped up. Like every other part of retirement, legacy needs a plan too.

◆◆◆◆◆

How do you want to be remembered, and by whom is it important to be remembered by?

Your Obituary

Take a moment and imagine your funeral—not to be morbid, but to reflect. What would you want your obituary to say? The typical biographical information has been laid out. Your education, occupation, and those who mourn your death are listed. Now, what would you like it to say about you? Or what would you want a couple of close

L = Live for Legacy

family members and friends to say about you? Author Steven Covey calls this *beginning with the end in mind*. If you document how others should think of you when you're gone, then you have a goal to reach while living. It doesn't have to be a full-blown obituary—think in terms of bullet points. Here are the bullet points I wrote for my obituary or the speakers at my funeral:

- She used her gifts and abilities to help others, leaving a positive and lasting impact on everyone she encountered.
- She lived by her priorities: God, family, self, community.
- She was generous with her time and money.
- She loved deeply.
- She gave without expectation of anything in return.
- She laughed a lot and found joy in life, even when things were difficult.
- She was the best mom and Mimi she could be.
- She died empty. This means she held nothing back but gave everything God called her to give.

I could list a dozen more points, but you get the idea. These become essential to driving my actions so I can leave the legacy I choose. As I take on new things in retirement, I ask myself, "How does this fit into my legacy?"

Now, it's your turn. What's essential for you? What are the values that you want people to remember about you? Who is critical to affect?

Your Legacy

You have an idea of the end, and now you can craft a legacy that fits these values. Here are a few steps that can be completed in any order:

1. What lessons have you learned in your 30 or 40 years of working? Can you share them with someone who will be coming behind you?
2. What values can you share with someone in your sphere of influence?
3. Who in your universe can you share these lessons with?
4. What deliberate methods will you take to share these lessons or values?

> 💡 **Pro Tip:. A fillable PDF is also available in the full workbook or at www.retiredandkillinit.com.**

Let's consider a few examples:

- Aaron, the CEO of a software company, will retire in one year. He has started to plan his second act and sees his legacy as a significant part of that. He's

L = Live for Legacy

not interested in a part-time job but having spent forty years of his career in the tech industry, he understands how to navigate it, and he wants to share that knowledge with others. Aaron connects with a few young tech executives on LinkedIn and establishes a small mentoring group, hosting a one-hour monthly forum to answer questions and provide advice. Aaron's impact will continue long after he retires because he has shared valuable experiences and wisdom.

- Natalie recently retired after a thirty-five-year career with the government. She is a single woman with no children but has a large family and many nieces, nephews, and young cousins. Natalie highly values family and believes in the importance of a cohesive family. She undertakes the creation of the family tree and engages her younger family members to help with researching their family history. Twice a month, she has a Zoom call with several nieces and nephews to discuss the findings and work on plans to present the family tree and detailed stories at the next family reunion. Natalie will be remembered as the person who dedicated time to documenting and preserving the family history.

How will you continue sharing what you've learned with others? Maybe you're a good cook. In this microwave-focused, fast-food generation, you have a much-needed skill and could teach a small cooking class to young adults (and older adults—I'll sign up). I know many people who enjoy reading. Imagine volunteering at a library and passing on your love of reading to children.

For many of us, legacy isn't just about what we leave behind—it's also about who we're becoming and why we're here. Retirement gives us the time and space to reflect on those deeper questions and align our actions with what truly matters.

Spiritual Legacy

For people of faith, retirement is a season of listening for spiritual direction, living with greater intention, and focusing on impact that aligns with eternal value, such as serving others, mentoring, or living out one's faith more fully. You might see this as your opportunity to serve in ministry, deepen your prayer life, or walk more closely in your calling.

For others, the spiritual side may show up as a sense of purpose, a desire to contribute to something bigger than oneself. That could mean volunteering, mentoring, caring for others, advocating for justice, or stewarding your gifts in a new way.

L = Live for Legacy

Whatever your beliefs, this chapter of life can be about alignment with your values, your purpose, God, or your community. If your retirement plan is part of God's bigger plan for your life, honor that. Create space to listen, reflect, and respond. Whether you term it a calling, an assignment, or simply "the next right thing," don't overlook the inner work that makes the outer work worthwhile.

Your legacy can be whatever you want it to be, but it's going to be something, even if that something is that you shared nothing with the world. Even silence leaves a mark. Plan to leave a legacy that truly represents who you are and remember: the greatest impact is never about us alone.

> **"Your legacy is what you do every day."**
> **—Maya Angelou**

I = Ignite Your Passion

(Pursue What Brings You Energy and Fulfillment)

What's something you can do for hours and lose track of time? Sure, social media and TV might come to mind—but I mean something that changes your energy when you talk about it. You'd do it for free, even though you'd rather be paid. For some of us, it's not easy to identify. For me, it was.

Although I spent my entire career in finance and accounting, I've always been passionate about helping others. One of my superpowers is problem-solving, so I get excited when a problem connects to a solution. In my leadership roles, I've always been a coach. I used to tell those reporting to me that 50% of my job was to help them succeed, but success was 100% of theirs. As a leader, I was committed not only to completing the assigned task but also to playing a part in helping people become their best selves, which is one of my passions. Executive coaching was a natural fit for me, although it took some retraining to shift from being the

I = Ignite Your Passion

problem solver to coaching my clients in finding solutions to their problems. While attaining my executive coaching certification, I learned about retirement coaching. I was already trained in retirement planning, but retirement coaching was a new concept. As I experienced my first few months of retirement, I felt something was missing. As a planner by nature, I realized my plan for my second act was not detailed. I had a general idea of what I might do: travel, spend time with my grandkids, consult, and coach a few clients, but there were no specifics. I had not answered the questions:

- What do I enjoy doing, and how much time do I want to spend doing that? I've been on a schedule for decades; it's my time to do things I enjoy.

- How much time would I spend coaching and consulting? I don't want it to feel like a full-time job.

- How much travel do I want to do? Although traveling frequently may sound appealing, it can affect your social rhythm and strain connections if you're always on the go.

I realized through retirement coaching that, with twenty to thirty years of life still ahead of them, most people enter this significant phase without a plan. As a result, it's not unusual for people to return to work after a few years because they are bored. If you're going to work in retirement, why not make it part of the plan and choose a role you'll enjoy? I enjoy executive coaching because I do it on my terms. I don't take on a lot of clients, and I engage only clients whom I'm confident I can help. Naturally, I want to be paid, but I don't do it for the money; otherwise, I'd take on any client.

Whether holding a physical copy of this book or reading it on a device, you're holding something I'm passionate about. I want everyone to be Retired and KILLIN' IT! I want everyone's second act to be more exciting and fun— or at least just as fulfilling as their first act. I want to erase the perception that retirement is doing just one thing: golfing, playing pickleball, or gardening. I am passionate about helping people discover the second act that feels like a reward for the hard push they made in the first act.

I watched my mom do this. After retiring, she started making jewelry. She began crafting earrings and necklaces, gifting them to friends and eventually selling them at local craft fairs. It wasn't about the money; it was about creating something with her hands, seeing people light up, and doing something that brought her true joy.

That's what passion looks like in retirement—it doesn't have to be big, flashy, or public. It just needs to feel good and keep you connected to yourself.

I = Ignite Your Passion

◆◆◆◆◆

Your Passion

So, let's return to the initial question: What's your passion? What is it that you get excited about doing?

- Are you an artist who loses yourself in your craft?
- Do you love organizing closets? That's a gift—use it.
- Are you a writer, and should you be writing a book or a blog?
- Do you love some sport and should find a club or join a 55+ league?
- Are you a gym enthusiast? Be an accountability partner?
- Do you love to walk? Could you join or start a walking club?
- Do you enjoy teaching? Where might you be able to teach and enjoy it?
- Do you love pets? How can you turn that love of pets into an opportunity to enjoy yourself?

> 💡 **Pro Tip:** Use the worksheet in the Appendix to guide you. A fillable PDF is also available in the full workbook or at www.retiredandkillinit.com.

Whatever your passion, there is a way to discover and ignite it. It doesn't mean every moment of the next twenty to thirty years will be rainbows and sunshine, but it does mean that you know the levers to pull that help you return joy to your routine when things get difficult.

Reflection Prompt:

- ✓ What are the top three activities or interests? that give you energy and make you feel most like yourself?
- ✓ How can you build more time into your life for one of them this month?

What's your passion? What is it that you get excited about doing?

N = Nurture Your Network
(Cultivate Meaningful and Inspiring Relationships)

While you were working—whether in an office, on the road, on your feet, or in a uniform—connecting with people happened naturally. You crossed paths with coworkers, clients, customers, patients, passengers, or partners. Some relationships were deep and lasting; others were built on routine and shared responsibilities. But when you retire, that rhythm shifts. The built-in connections fade, and staying meaningfully connected takes more effort. Now, you get to choose who's in your circle—and that choice is more important than ever.

Your networks won't look the same in retirement, and they shouldn't. That's because the purpose has changed. Your network isn't about your next job opportunity anymore, but your next chapter. And it matters more than ever, because this time, your network is about relationships, not contacts.

N = Nurture Your Network

While we are working, our networks include everyone from trusted colleagues to people we met once at a conference, even people we didn't know personally but were connected to through others. That web naturally kept growing. In retirement, those touchpoints shrink.

Even if you're aiming for a board seat or launching a consulting business, your network will shift—it'll need to be more focused and intentional. You no longer need a large network; you need to be deliberate. You need to identify the relationships that matter and nurture those.

That's why it's worth asking: Which relationships still matter? And what kind of connections will support your emotional, social, and psychological well-being in the future?

◆◆◆◆◆

Start by looking at four key circles that often shape your social world:

- Family
- Friends
- Former Coworkers
- Faith or Community Connections

Use the chart below as a self-check. Who lifts you up? Who drains you? Who deserves more of your time—and who might need less?

	Who is in this circle?	What role do they play in my life now?	What do I want more or less of in this relationship?	Do I want to grow, maintain, or let go?
Family				
Friends				
Coworkers				
Faith/ Community Connections				

Note: This list is not all-inclusive; you may have more relevant relationships to list in the left column.

Family

On the surface, this might seem like the most effortless transition. Your titles don't change just because you've retired—you're still a parent, grandparent, sibling, aunt, or uncle. However, retirement can shift the dynamics more than you expect.

- Your kids may assume you're always available for grandkid duty.
- Family might lean on you for items on their to-do list.
- And your ability to spend, give, or travel might look different now.

That's why it's worth stepping back and asking: What do I want these relationships to look like now? You might decide to nurture some, set boundaries with others, or even step back where needed. If your time is spent constantly meeting the needs of others, retirement can stop feeling like freedom and start feeling like another job, and you'll quickly wish you were back at work.

Caring for Aging Family Members

Now is also when many of us start caring for aging parents, in-laws, or even a spouse. It's real. It's demanding. And if you're not careful, it can take over.

The guilt hits hard, especially when the person you care for isn't enjoying life as you are. You've heard it before, but it's worth repeating: **You can't pour from an empty cup** or, as the airlines say, "Put on your mask before helping others."

You may not be able to take every trip or say yes to everything, but you still need a life and moments that are just for you.

1. *Take care of yourself.* This is the first thing to lose its place on the priority list. You become so focused on meeting the needs of the person you care for that you don't realize you've stopped meeting yours. One day, you look up, and you're not eating right; you've stopped exercising, and you look ten years older because you've allowed your needs to come last. Choose something just for you—a walk, the gym, lunch with friends, or a quiet hour alone—and protect it. Add it to your calendar like any other appointment.

2. *Ask for help.* You might be surprised by how many people would be willing to help if you simply let them. When my immediate family had an event and my Dad couldn't travel with us, we contacted cousins, friends, and my kids to take shifts visiting and checking on him. They showed up, and he loved seeing more people. There may be certain

N = Nurture Your Network

things you can't hand off, but there are things others can do if you let go of control and accept the support.

3. *Pay for help if you can.* This doesn't have to be expensive. College students, neighbors with flexible jobs, or individuals seeking a side hustle are good options to sit and play cards with your loved one, watch TV with them, or simply provide companionship. You'd be surprised how much a two-hour break can do for your energy and mindset. And with today's smart home cameras, you can keep an eye on things even when you're not there.

Here's a quick checklist to help you protect your peace while supporting the people you love:

- ✓ **Put yourself on your own calendar**
  Block time weekly for you—a walk, a workout, lunch with a friend, or just peace and quiet.

- ✓ **Say yes to support**
  Let people help. Whether it's family, friends, or neighbors, ask, accept, and delegate where you can.

- ✓ **Pay for help if you can**
  Even a couple of hours of companionship from a college student or neighbor can give you a real reset.

- ✓ **Don't disappear**
  Stay social. Caregiving can be isolating, but a simple coffee catch-up can refill your tank.
- ✓ **Monitor your health**
  Exhaustion, weight changes, mood swings—don't ignore them. Your well-being matters just as much.

> 💡 **Pro Tip:** Drop this list in your calendar as a weekly reminder. Taking care of you isn't selfish—it's smart.

Family relationships may be the most familiar, but they're not the only ones that shape your retirement. If you want joy, energy, and connection in this next chapter of your life, you need the right people around you. That's where your friendships come in.

Friends

Friendships can shift in retirement because so many parts of life change. If you move, or if your friend group was tied to work, that regular rhythm of connection can fade. Even if you're in the same city, your schedules or priorities may not align as they used to. The good news is you've got more time now—but you may need to be more intentional about how and with whom you spend it, especially if your friends have not yet retired.

N = Nurture Your Network

Friendships can feed the spirit, but not all friendships are equal. Knowing which friendships you want to invest your time and energy in is essential. I categorize friendships into four levels. I envision them as boxes of varying sizes.

1. **Acquaintances**—superficial interaction
2. **Casual**—more contact, common interest with a safe distance
3. **Close**—share similar life goals, discuss hard questions, socialize, exercise, and vacation together
4. **Intimate**—regular contact and deep commitment, open and vulnerable. These are the people you turn to for guidance, honesty, and encouragement. Intimate friends are as free to criticize and to correct you as they are to embrace and encourage you because trust and a mutual understanding have been established.

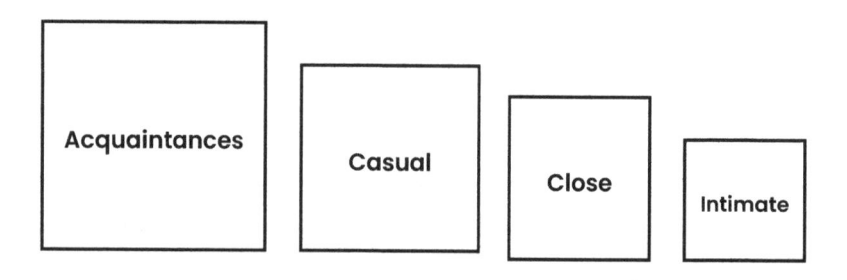

Not everyone belongs in the same box—and that last one, the "intimate friend" box, should be Tiffany-box small.

Why? Because deeply trusted friendships are rare. These categories help you protect your energy, especially now that your time is your own.

The largest box? Acquaintances—people you know, maybe chat with, but don't go deep. Some of them will move closer over time. The catch? We sometimes treat casual friends like close ones. When expectations don't match reality, disappointment follows. Friendships naturally shift forward or backward. Friction happens when we try to force someone to stay where they don't belong anymore.

This evaluation of friendships can easily spill over into your work relationships because many coworkers start as acquaintances but, over time, develop into casual or close friends. It is the rare person who finds their BFF (best friend forever) at work.

Former Coworkers

We have all types of relationships when we are working, and when we retire, those relationships change. We have good intentions of staying in touch with everyone we've ever liked at work, but **grass grows where it's watered**. Many coworker relationships are not significant or deep enough that we intentionally water them. In the retirement honeymoon phase, we're scheduling lunches, swapping texts, and promising to keep in touch, but coworkers are busy and still in the trenches, and that responsiveness can trail off.

Using the table presented earlier to evaluate your relationships, you can identify the coworkers who are vital to maintain connections with and create an accountability plan for how you will do that. You'll develop new relationships in your retired life, and if you are going to work in retirement, you may have a different network.

However, maintaining connections with former coworkers has value both in the friendships you've developed and in connecting to the work you may continue in retirement. Past coworkers can become your biggest champions when you're stepping into something new—they've seen you deliver.

Faith/Community Connections

Most people volunteer for something, whether it's in the community or at their church. Having more time for community and faith work means you will have more time to invest in the relationships, but the question is, which relationships do you want to invest in? These two groups are part of your post-retirement network, and identifying which of those relationships are worthy of deeper investment helps you use your time and energy wisely. These relationships—whether through your church, volunteer circles, or community work—are often the ones that shape your legacy (See Chapter 6). They're not just about staying connected; they're about staying impactful.

Whether deepening family bonds, reconnecting with old colleagues, or forging new friendships in your community, nurturing your network isn't just about staying social; it's about choosing who receives your energy and ensuring that those relationships reflect the life you're building in retirement.

Once you've taken stock of the people around you, the next step is deciding how you'll show up for them. Because this chapter isn't just about who's around you—it's about who you choose to show up for.

Now, you get to choose who's in your circle—and that choice is more important than ever.

I = Invest in Others
(Share Knowledge and Give Back)

Retirement doesn't mean you're done giving—it means you finally get to choose *how* you give.

For years, your energy went into someone else's goals—your boss's, your team's, your company's. Now, you get to choose where that energy goes, and who benefits from it.

"Investing in others" isn't just about staying busy—it's about doing something that matters. It's about giving your time, your wisdom, and your encouragement in ways that help someone else grow. Legacy is what you leave behind. Investing in others is what you do now. One sparks the fire. The other is what's left burning.

One of the challenges in retirement is questioning your relevancy. The question isn't whether you're still relevant—it's who you're trying to be relevant to. Your old title? Your calendar? Or something deeper? When you pour into others, whether by mentoring, teaching, listening, or just showing up, you stop worrying about being essential and

I = Invest in Others

focus on being useful. That's what makes this chapter so powerful. This is a mental shift in how you've operated for years.

You don't have to launch a nonprofit or run a program. Sometimes, investing in others just means being present. Maybe you teach someone a skill. Perhaps you speak positively into someone who's struggling. Or you can just listen.

I have a friend who retired from the state police as a highranking officer. Not long after, she began volunteering at a women's minimum-security prison, teaching life skills and preparing women for successful reentry into society. She tapped into her passion for supporting women, many of whom had struggled with addiction or criminal records, helping them reclaim their lives. What she shared wasn't just shaped by her career—it was real-life wisdom from raising sons, facing adversity, and choosing growth.

◆◆◆◆◆

Reflection: Take a moment to think about this: Who in your life could use your time, your ear, your story, or your skills right now?

_____

_____

_____

_____

_____

- ✓ Offer to mentor someone just starting out
- ✓ Teach a grandchild to cook a family recipe
- ✓ Join a local volunteer program
- ✓ Help a young adult with resume or college prep
- ✓ Help a neighbor with a task they're struggling with
- ✓ Sit with an older adult and listen to their stories
- ✓ Support a caregiver by offering them a break

One of the most overlooked but meaningful ways to invest in others is to show up for your aging parents or older relatives. According to the Pew Research Center, as many as 71% of Baby Boomers have one parent living.[15] A 2012 report by Ameriprise Financial revealed that 60% of Boomers are assisting an aging parent in some way.[16] Many entering retirement will devote significant time to caring for their parents. And really, who better to invest in than the one who's invested in you your whole life?

I = Invest in Others

You can invest in your aging parent and even share your knowledge in multiple ways:

- ✓ Listening to their stories (even when they're repeating them)
- ✓ Including them in your joy (take them along with you on your journeys)
- ✓ Help them stay connected (technology can be frustrating; help them connect with friends and grandkids)
- ✓ Respecting what still matters to them (honor their routine, pride, and preferences)
- ✓ Speak life into them (tell them why they still matter, remind them what they've given you)

These moments may not appear to involve service, but they're sacred. And they matter. Even in caregiving, you're modeling what it looks like to love well, which might be the most powerful investment.

Investing in others isn't just about what you give—it's about what you gain. It reminds you that you still matter, even without a title or a paycheck. And if you keep investing in yourself and others, you'll keep KILLIN' IT. Own that.

T = Tell Yourself You Are KILLIN' IT
(Own Your Retirement)

You've done a lot of work to get here.

Remember back in Chapter 1, when you asked yourself, "What's my 'why'?", and in Chapter 2, when you peeled back the layers of identity—from titles to roles to who you really are? Look at how far you've come.

You started with questions. Now, you've built a plan. You mapped out your ideal week, reimagined your purpose, found your passions, and even dared yourself to do something bold. That's not just growth, that's reinvention.

Retirement is not the end of your identity. It's a chance to align who you are with how you live—fully, freely, and on your terms. You've done the hard work of reflection, and now it's time to execute.

No matter how good your KILLIN' IT plan is, you are the only person who can make it truly rock. You can have the perfect plan, all the time in the world, and a bucket list ready to go—but if your mindset doesn't match the life you're trying to build it will all be a bust. This chapter is about how you talk to yourself, how you see yourself, and how you own the truth. This isn't just retirement—it's your next season. It's the time in your life when you can do almost ANYTHING you want.

I say "almost" because sure, there are a few limits. But don't let them become excuses. I read about retirees in their 80s running marathons. If your first thought is, "I can't do that," ask yourself, "How do I know?" For me, running a marathon isn't a limit—it's just a "don't want to." And that's the beauty of retirement. It's about choosing the "want to." The grandson of a friend of mine once said, "I can't want to." That is an excellent response for me in retirement.

When Life Throws a Curveball

But even with the best mindset and a great plan, life will interrupt. Because that's what life does. You can have your "KILLIN' IT" dashboard filled out, your vision board taped to the wall, and your suitcase packed for the next adventure—and then the unexpected happens. Maybe it's a health scare. A loved one's diagnosis. A financial hit. The loss of someone close.

In those moments, your plan may feel irrelevant. But here's the truth: Your plan isn't just for when life is smooth. It's your anchor when everything gets messy. The KILLIN' IT formula isn't rigid. It flexes.

Some chapters in your life may be heavy on "Invest in Others" or "Keep Moving." At other times, you may lean into "Laugh a Lot" just to get through the day. The point is not to be perfect. The point is to keep showing up—even if the pace slows or the priorities shift.

And when life knocks the wind out of you? Pause. Grieve. Breathe.

Then ask yourself:

- What do I still have in this moment?
- What do I need to take care of myself right now?
- And when I'm ready, how do I take one small step back toward joy?

Retirement Is a Journey, Not a Destination

If you've made it this far, here's what I hope you know by now: **Retirement isn't one big moment—it's thousands of little ones**. It's not a finish line; it's a new course. Some days will be smooth. Some days, you'll question whether you're doing it right. That's normal. You're learning a new rhythm—and the learning never stops.

T = Tell Yourself You Are KILLIN' IT

The art of KILLIN' IT is personal. You might look at my life in retirement and say it's not for you or that I'm doing too much. Retirement for you might entail digging in your garden or reading at the beach. I despise dirt under my fingernails, bugs anywhere near me, and abhor sand in my clothes. But I love this for you. Whatever you want to do in retirement, make a plan and make it happen. And don't measure it against someone else's life. Measure it against the values and vision that matter to you.

Don't Forget Your Retirement Tagline

What's the phrase that sums up your new chapter? A mantra. A mindset. A one-liner that says: "This is how I'm showing up in this season"?

Mine? ***"I'm Retired and KILLIN' IT."***

Yours might be:

- "More naps, less nonsense."
- "Booked, busy, and blessed."
- "Work optional, joy required."

Write it down. Tape it to the mirror. Let it guide your choices.

Even When You Don't Feel Like You're KILLIN' IT . . .

Some days, it's easy to feel like you're KILLIN' IT, and other days, not so much. But here's where it counts… Tell yourself you are. Why? Because your attitude impacts your altitude. You don't have to fake perfection. However, you need to remind yourself of your power, especially when you're feeling off. It's not about pretending everything's great. It's about keeping your foot on the gas, even if you're only going 10 mph today.

One of the biggest shifts in retirement is how quiet the praise becomes. There are no more awards for going above and beyond, no Employee of the Month plaques, no staff announcements, or big thank-you emails. When you do something amazing now—like tackling a long-postponed goal, helping someone out, or just making it through a tough week—the applause might come from your family, a couple of friends, and maybe the seventeen people who like your Facebook or LinkedIn post. And that's if you even share it. However, the cheering section was never as important as you thought. Truth is, even if the cheering section says you nailed it—if you don't believe it, their praise won't stick. And if they miss it, but you know you crushed it? That's what matters most. You need to believe it

T = Tell Yourself You Are KILLIN' IT

yourself. Look yourself in the mirror and say with as much attitude and confidence as you can: **I'M KILLIN' IT!**

Celebrate YOU

Take a second and look at where you are. Seriously. You've navigated a career, a family, life's curveballs, and now you're here, building something new. That deserves a moment. Light a candle. Take yourself out for dinner. Blast your favorite song. Fire up the grill for no reason. Frame the moment with a photo. Dance like no one's watching. Whatever joy looks like for you, DO THAT. Every time you do something that makes you smile, or accomplish something you didn't think you could, celebrate. I crossed three countries off my bucket list in my first year of retirement. I feel great about that—and I'm not shy about saying it: I'm KILLIN' IT.

Sharing Your Story

Your story matters, so share it over coffee, on social media, or with your grandkids. Someone needs to hear what retirement looks like from your point of view. Someone needs to know they're not the only ones trying to figure it out. Your experience could be the encouragement someone else is waiting for. So please don't keep it to yourself.

The first time I used the phrase "I'm KILLIN' IT" as it relates to retirement was at the mPowering YOU conference. I was amazed how many people approached me after that panel and wanted to discuss my retirement story. At the time, I had only been retired for three weeks, but several people said they had never seen someone so excited about their retirement. Get excited about yours and share that excitement. Imagine being in a group with excited retired people. If you've found one, hold on tight and share with others.

◆◆◆◆◆

Your Retirement Dashboard

Want to keep track of how you're KILLIN' IT? Create a simple visual aid that helps you stay on track. Maybe it's a pie chart of how you spend your time (like in Chapter 4). Maybe it's a monthly "joy tracker"—one thing that lit you up each week.

Or a simple checklist:

- ✓ Did something for myself
- ✓ Moved my body
- ✓ Laughed out loud
- ✓ Showed up for someone
- ✓ Tried something new

T = *Tell Yourself You Are KILLIN' IT*

Below is a simple example of a dashboard. Your dashboard should be whatever works for you and helps with accountability.

Retirement Dashboard	
Retirement Factor	**Week 1**
Keep Moving	
Imagine What's Next	
Laugh a Lot	
Live for Legacy	
Ignite Your Passion	
Nurture Your Network	
Invest in Others	
Tell Yourself You Are Killin' It	

This is less about the metrics and more about the mindset. You don't need to hit every box every day. You just need a way to stay accountable to your intention. If you show up for your life with intention and joy, you're doing just fine.

Retirement is yours now. Own it. Define it. Live it with joy and intention. And whatever comes next—just keep **KILLIN' IT.**

> **DAILY AFFIRMATION:**
> This is my time.
> My plan.
> My pace.
> And I'M KILLIN' IT.

T = Tell Yourself You Are KILLIN' IT

Before You Close the Book...

Thank you for letting me walk this journey with you. Whether you're already retired or just starting to imagine it, I hope this book helped you see retirement not as an end, but as an invitation.

We've explored the KILLIN' IT Formula—not as a checklist, but as a mindset shift.

K	= Keep Moving
I	= Imagine What's Next
L	= Laugh a Lot
L	= Live for Legacy
I	= Ignite Your Passion
N	= Nurture Your Network
I	= Invest in Others
T	= Tell Yourself You Are KILLIN' It

Final Reflection:

Are you ready to move forward but not sure where to start?

- Pick one part of the KILLIN' IT Formula to focus on first.
- Create a working group and build your plans together.

- Visit www.retiredandkillinit.com for the PDF fillable workbook or sign up for a workshop.

Retirement is a long chapter. Make it your best one yet.

Retirement isn't one big moment—it's thousands of little ones.

PART 3:
Worksheets

APPENDIX:
Retired and KILLIN' IT Worksheets

This appendix contains a sample of worksheets designed to help you reflect, reimagine, and redefine your retirement journey. Use them at your own pace and revisit them.

A complete workbook of fillable forms is available at www.retiredandkillinit.com

There's still a next chapter waiting to be written, BY YOU.

Chapter 2 – Identity & Reinvention

From What → To What Identity Map

1. Who I was (Title, Role, Identity):

2. Who am I becoming (New identity, Values, Direction):

3. I want to be seen as someone who:

This isn't about status—it's about creating meaning, joy, and connection with what you have, where you are.

Chapter 4 – Imagine What's Next

Getting Creative with Retirement – Your Possibilities, Bucket and Dare Lists

Possibilities	Bucket	Dare

Plan to leave a legacy that truly represents who you are.

Chapter 5 – Legacy Builder

Worksheet: Obituary Bullets + Legacy Actions

If someone gave a eulogy for me today, I'd want them to say:

Now, here's how I'll live that legacy:

Most people enter this significant phase without a plan.

Chapter 7 - Ignite Your Passion Worksheet

Use this worksheet to reflect on what truly excites you in retirement. Your answers can guide how you spend your time and energy in this next chapter.

1. **Passion Reflection**

What three activities or interests give you energy and make you feel most like yourself?

1.
2.
3.

How can you build more time for one of them this month?

2. **What Makes You Feel Alive?**

What is something you could do for hours and lose track of time?

Whatever your passion, there is a way to discover and ignite it.

What would you do even if no one paid you, simply because you love it?

3. Try Something New

What's one thing you've always wanted to try, but haven't yet?

What's holding you back?

Nurturing your network isn't just about staying social; it's about choosing who receives your energy.

Chapter 8 – Relationship Audit Table

	Who is in this circle?	What role do they play in my life now?	What do I want more or less of in this relationship?	Do I want to grow, maintain, or let go?
Family				
Friends				
Coworkers				
Faith/ Community Connections				

Retirement is yours now. Own it. Define it. Live it with joy and intention.

Chapter 10 – Your Retirement Dashboard

Retirement Dashboard	
Retirement Factor	**Week 1**
Keep Moving	
Imagine What's Next	
Laugh a Lot	
Live for Legacy	
Ignite Your Passion	
Nurture Your Network	
Invest in Others	
Tell Yourself You Are Killin' It	

Endnotes

1. Thomas H. Holmes and Richard H. Rahe, "The Social Readjustment Rating Scale," *Journal of Psychosomatic Research* 11, no. 2 (1967): 213–218. https://doi.org/10.1016/0022-3999(67)90010-4

2. Helen R. Ebaugh, *Becoming an Ex: The Process of Role Exit* (Chicago: University of Chicago Press, 1998).

3. Elisabeth Kübler-Ross, *On Death and Dying* , 50th Anniversary ed, (New York: Scribner, 2014).

4. The accompanying workbook can be found at https://www.retiredandkillinit.com.

5. Fritz Gilbert, "The Dark Side of Retirement," *Retirement Manifesto*, November 19, 2019, https://www.theretirementmanifesto.com/the-dark-side-of-retirement/

6. "How Common is Depression in Older Adults?" *National Council on Aging*, September 11, 2024, https://www.ncoa.org/article/how-common-is-depression-in-older-adults/

7. Taylor Shuman, "A Guide to Substance Abuse in Older Adults: Risks, Warning Signs, and Treatments," April 18, 2025, https://www.seniorliving.org/research/substance-abuse-seniors/

8. Candy Sagon, "Stay Active: Physical Decline Starts Earlier Than Thought," *AARP*, August 25, 2016, https://www.aarp.org/health/healthy-living/fitness-aging-physical-decline/

9. "Older Adults with Declining Physical Function at Greater Risk of Dying," *National Institute on Aging*, October 28, 2021, https://www.nia.nih.gov/news/older-adults-declining-physical-function-greater-risk-dying

10. Rachel A. Tee-Melegrito, "How to Prevent Heart Disease," *Medical News Today*, February 28, 2023, https://www.medicalnewstoday.com/articles/327021

11. "Is Taking 10,000 Steps a Day Necessary for Optimal Health?" *Mount Sinai Today*, May 5, 2023, https://health.mountsinai.org/blog/is-taking-10000-steps-a-day-necessary-for-optimal-health/

12. Robert Laura, Dorian Mintzer, and Gillian Leithman, *Certified Professional Retirement Coach Course Manual* (unpublished manuscript, 2018), 180, https://certifiedretirementcoach.org/

13. Robert Laura, Dorian Mintzer, and Gillian Leithman, *Certified Professional Retirement Coach Course Manual* (unpublished manuscript, 2018), 34, https://certifiedretirementcoach.org/

14. Charles R. Swindoll, *Life Is 10% What Happens to You and 90% How You React: Cultivating Inner Strength and Embracing Hope When Life is Not What You Expected* (Nashville: Thomas Nelson, 2023).

15. "Baby Boomers: From the Age of Aquarius to the Age of Responsibility," *Pew Research Center,* December 8, 2025, https://www.pewresearch.org/social-trends/2005/12/08/baby-boomers-from-the-age-of-aquarius-to-the-age-of-responsibility/

16. "Ameriprise: Boomers Put Families' Financial Needs First," *Twin Cities Business*, May 11, 2012, https://tcbmag.com/ameriprise-boomers-put-families-financial-needs-first/

About the Author

Lisa J. Haynes is an author, speaker, certified executive and retirement coach, and CEO of Haynes Executive Solutions. Lisa blends financial expertise with a deep commitment to personal growth and transformation.

Before retiring from her corporate role as Chief Financial Officer and Chief Diversity and Inclusion Officer, Lisa had already developed a passion for helping others' live with intention. As a published author and speaker, she built a platform rooted in authenticity, faith, and lifelong reinvention. After more than three decades in finance leadership, she made the leap into her second act—guiding others through their transitions with clarity, confidence, and purpose.

Today, Lisa supports individuals and organizations through her boutique firm with executive coaching, retirement strategy, and financial consulting. Her latest work, *Retired and Killin' It*, challenges the outdated notion that retirement is a winding down. Instead, it's a powerful reset—a launch pad for purpose, impact, and joy.

Known for her humor, heart, and unapologetic realness, Lisa is a mother, grandmother, mentor, and woman of faith. She continues to use her voice to inspire others to lead boldly in whatever chapter they're in.

To inquire about speaking engagements, visit https://www.retiredandkillinit.com/speaker-profile.